The Library of
# NATIVE AMERICANS

# The Lenape

*of Pennsylvania, New Jersey, New York, Delaware,*
*Wisconsin, Oklahoma, and Ontario*

## Anne Dalton

The Rosen Publishing Group's
**PowerKids Press**™
New York

*For Bella Myong-wol—your patience and curiosity guided me in this task*

Special thanks to James Rementer

Published in 2005 by The Rosen Publishing Group, Inc.
29 East 21st Street, New York, NY 10010

Photo and Illustration Credits: Cover, pp. 6, 12, 14, 35 The Lenni Lenape Historical Society/Museum of Indian Culture (www.lenape.org); p. 4, Mindy Liu; pp. 9, 26, 30, 43 Hulton Archive / Getty Images; pp. 11, 13 Lenape Lifeways Inc.; pp. 17, 21 Atwater Kent Museum of Philadelphia / Bridgeman Art Library; p. 18 The Study of the Delaware Indian Big House Ceremony, Frank Speck, Pennsylvania Historical and Museum Commission, 1931; pp. 22, 24 Courtesy of the Reading Public Museum, Reading, Pennsylvania; p. 33 New Netherland Institute, New York State Library; p. 36 Picture Collection, The Branch Libraries, The New York Public Library, Astor, Lenox and Tilden Foundations; p. 39 Independence National Historical Park; p. 40 Courtesy of the Pennsylvania Academy of the Fine Arts, Philadelphia. Gift of Mrs. Sarah Harrison (The Joseph Harrison, Jr. Collection), p. 45 © Bettman/Corbis; p. 48 Photo by Jim Rementer of Drum Studio original; p. 52 Courtesy of the Chemung County Historical Society, Inc., Elmira, New York; p. 53 Photo by Jim Rementer; pp. 54-55 © Bob Krist/CORBIS

Book Design: Erica Clendening
Book Layout, Lenape Art, and Production: Mindy Liu
Contributing Editor: Shira Laskin

Library of Congress Cataloging-in-Publication Data

Dalton, Anne.
   The Lenape of Pennsylvania, New Jersey, New York, Delaware, Wisconsin,
   Oklahoma, and Ontario / Anne Dalton.— 1st ed.
   p. cm. — (The library of Native Americans)
   Includes index.
   Contents: Introducing the Lenape — Lenape technology — Lenape spirits and religion
   —Encounters with Europeans — The Lenape today.
   ISBN 1-4042-2872-1 (lib. bdg.)
   1. Delaware Indians—History—Juvenile literature. 2. Delaware Indians—Social life
   and customs—Juvenile literature. [1. Delaware Indians. 2. Indians of North America
   Middle Atlantic States.] I. Title. II. Series.

   E99.D2D16 2005
   974.004'97345—dc22
                                    2003025406

*Manufactured in the United States of America*

*There are a variety of terminologies that have been employed when writing about Native Americans. There are sometimes differences between the original language used by a Native American group for certain names or vocabulary and the anglicized or modernized versions of such names or terms. Although this book contains terms that we feel will be most recognizable to our readership, there may also exist synonymous or native words that are preferred by certain speakers.*

The creation myth on page 28 is a retelling by Heinz Insu Fenkl of the tale originally collected by Adrien Vander Donck between 1641 and 1655 and is used with the author's permission.

# Contents

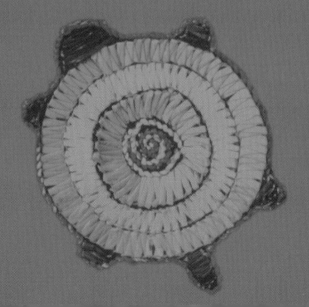

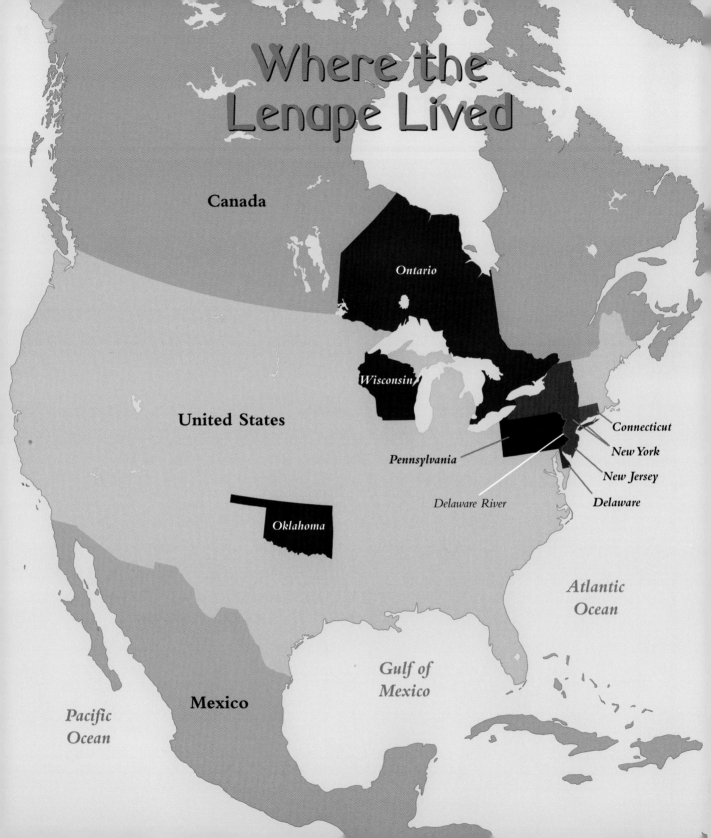

# Where the Lenape Lived

Canada

Ontario

Wisconsin

United States

Pennsylvania

Connecticut

New York

New Jersey

Delaware River

Delaware

Oklahoma

Atlantic Ocean

Gulf of Mexico

Mexico

Pacific Ocean

# One

## Introducing the Lenape

It was long before the subways and skyscrapers of Manhattan and Newark took shape and long before anyone dreamed of building the Statue of Liberty. It was a time when the waters of the Atlantic Ocean and the Hudson River overflowed with fish such as shad, sturgeon, and bass, and when much of North America seemed like a land of endless forests. It was the time of the Lenape.

## Origin of the Lenape

Most scholars believe that people from Asia came to North America around 40,000 years ago by crossing a frozen land bridge that stretched from Siberia to Alaska. These people were the ancestors of the Native Americans. They slowly moved south, inhabiting different parts of North and South America. By about 12,000 years ago, some of them had reached the tip of South America. Very little is known about these first Americans.

The Lenape lived in many areas, including New Jersey, Delaware, Pennsylvania, New York, and later in Oklahoma, Wisconsin, and Ontario, Canada.

6     The Lenape used porcupine quills to make baskets and to decorate clothing and bags. The quills were hollow and were threaded like beads. Sometimes the quills were dyed or flattened before they were used.

# Understanding the Lenape

For the past thousand years, and perhaps far longer, the Lenape hunted as far north as the Catskill Mountains and as far south as the Delaware Bay. Some of the Lenape were river dwellers, some lived on the coast, and others lived in forests. All Lenape shared cultural traditions and common language roots.

Lenapehoking, the land of the Lenape, covered a vast area. This included all of New Jersey, part of Delaware, eastern Pennsylvania, southeastern New York State (including Staten Island and part of western Long Island), parts of Oklahoma and Ontario, and a small part of southwestern Connecticut. The ocean, rivers, forests, mountains, valleys, and streams between the Hudson and Delaware River valleys, from New York Bay to Delaware Bay, were all part of the Lenape homeland.

The Lenape did not consider themselves to be part of a single nation or unified tribe. Along with the Mahicans and other native peoples, the Lenape were part of a larger group called the Algonquians. This group was not linked by a central leader or government. Groups lived separately, but they shared common values, traditions, family structure, and spiritual practices.

The language spoken by the Lenape was a part of the Algonquian language family, with three distinct dialects. Those in the northernmost groups spoke the Munsee dialect. The word Munsee means "the people of the stony country." These Lenape lived along the Hudson River, in Pennsylvania, New Jersey, and along the beginning of the Delaware River.

Two other dialects spoken by the Lenape were Southern and Northern Unami. Unami means "the people downriver." These dialects were spoken by the Lenape living along the Delaware River, through central and southern New Jersey, and parts of Pennsylvania and Delaware.

The Lenape had a position of importance among the Algonquian-speaking tribes. Other tribes often called the Lenape "grandfathers." This was a sign of deep respect. Many Algonquians believed the Lenape were the original tribe of all Algonquian-speaking people.

The name Lenape has several meanings, including "real people," "ordinary people," and "common people." The Lenape have also been called many names by those outside of the tribe. They were called Easterners by Algonquian-speaking people who lived farther west. They were later called *Loups*, which means wolves, by the French. This is perhaps because a central Lenape clan is the wolf clan.

Today, the Lenape fight to keep their culture alive. Years of European invasion of their homeland have left them scattered across North America. They are now known mostly as the Delaware and the Munsee tribes. However, despite all the Lenape have endured their traditions live on.

This drawing of a Lenape couple was done by a Swedish explorer named Peter Lindestrom, who encountered the Lenape in the 1640s.

# Two
# Lenape Technology

## Food

The activities of the Lenape changed with the seasons. During the spring, they caught fish, such as shad and alewives. The Lenape made dugout canoes to travel through fishing waters. These were boats made from hollowed-out tree trunks. They did most of their fishing with handwoven nets that they made from a plant called hemp. To preserve food for the colder seasons, the Lenape smoked large quantities of the fish that they caught. They did this by exposing the fish to smoke for long periods of time.

In the coastal areas of Lenapehoking, archaeologists, or scientists who study the past, have uncovered huge piles of shells. These shells show that clams, oysters, and other shellfish were also a source of food for some Lenape. Eels and turtles were a part of their diet as well. Often, the Lenape used leftover parts of the animals they ate to make tools, decorative jewelry, and musical instruments for different ceremonies. Oyster and snail shells were made into beads. The Lenape used clamshells as spoons. They made turtle shells into rattles for ceremonies and healing rituals.

The Lenape used dugout canoes to travel on lakes, rivers, and possibly even the ocean. The canoes were carved from the trunks of tulip, elm, oak, and chestnut trees.

Late spring and early summer were the time for planting, fishing, gathering wild grains and vegetables, and hunting. Corn, which the Lenape called *xas-kweem*, became a central part of the tribe's diet about 1,000 years ago. The corn they grew was small and had blue, red, white, and gold kernels. Squash and beans were also a key source of food. Once the corn plants started growing, the Lenape planted beans, which would grow up and around the corn stalks for support. The Lenape also planted summer and winter squash among the beans and corn. The leafy vines of each of these plants helped

**12** The Lenape often cooked their food in clay pots, such as these found in the Lehigh Valley in Pennsylvania.

keep the soil moist. Much of the harvest was stored for late fall, winter, and early spring when food sources were scarce. Squash, corn, beans, and other foods such as berries, roots, nuts, and meats were dried. Dried foods could be stored and eaten over the winter and during the spring thaw, as the ground began to warm up.

Along with their duties of collecting firewood, sewing clothes, and making pottery, Lenape women grew, gathered, stored, and prepared most of the food. They had many cooking methods, which included heating food in clay pots and roasting food in fires. The Lenape prepared their corn in many different ways. They ate it raw, boiled it in water, and roasted it over a fire. Often, they ate it in the form of a cornmeal mush called *sapan. Sapan* was an important part of the Lenape diet. The Lenape used a mortar in which they ground the corn into cornmeal, or a coarsely ground corn flour. The cornmeal was then mixed with wet ingredients to form the *sapan.*

This is the type of mortar and pestle used by the Lenape to make *sapan.*

# Hunting

Hunting was a year-round activity performed mostly by men. Fall and winter hunts were especially important. Although the Lenape ate many smoked and dried foods stored from spring and summer,

14 Hunting was an important part of Lenape life. Animals such as deer, elk, and bison were a part of the Lenape diet during the colder part of the year. The larger of the two bones pictured above is believed to be the shoulder bone of a deer. The arrowhead that killed the animal remains in the bone. The origin of the smaller bone is unknown.

animal protein and fat were an important part of their diet during the colder months when fresh food was scarce.

The Lenape hunted using spears, bows and arrows, or more elaborate methods, such as fire surrounds. Using this technique, the Lenape burned the trees in a part of a forest to trap animals in that area. The Lenape hunted large mammals, such as deer, bison, elk, and bear. They also ate raccoons, geese, turkey, and squirrels.

The winter was also a busy and productive time for those who did not hunt. This was the time when the Lenape gathered in lodges to make the items they needed for everyday life. They made clothes, tools, storage containers, and other items essential for food preparation. The winter was also a time for entertaining each other with stories. Lenape stories were passed on through generations as a part of their rich oral tradition.

# Tools

The Lenape were highly skilled toolmakers. They used stone, clay, bone, shell, wood, and other materials to make beautifully designed objects. The Lenape created a wide range of tools for cutting, chopping, pounding, piercing, drilling, scraping, and grinding.

By carefully flaking and chipping stone, the Lenape made spearheads, arrow points, scrapers, and knives. They also made axe heads, hammer stones, and net sinkers, which were important tools used to fish. Everything the Lenape used, from fishhooks to

15

war clubs, was made by hand from natural resources. Many Lenape toolmakers created detailed designs on their tools. Their work resulted in highly useful tools that were also extraordinary works of art.

# Shelter

The Lenape lived in bark lodges called wigwams. To build these lodges, very young hickory, elm, and chestnut trees were stripped, bent, and tied to form a frame. Other young trees were then added across the frame for support. Sheets of bark, sometimes six feet (1.83 m) long, were secured to the frame with flexible strips of inner bark. These sheets were arranged in overlapping patterns to help keep out wet and cold weather. Wigwams did not have windows and often had just one entrance. Smoke holes were left open in the roof to allow smoke from cooking hearths to escape.

There were storage areas at each end of these homes. The Lenape hung dried food, tobacco, and other supplies from the ceiling. Lenape wigwams had sleeping platforms that were also used as benches. Wigwams varied widely in size, from small oval or round buildings for a single family, to large oval lodges. These larger lodges could house many related families.

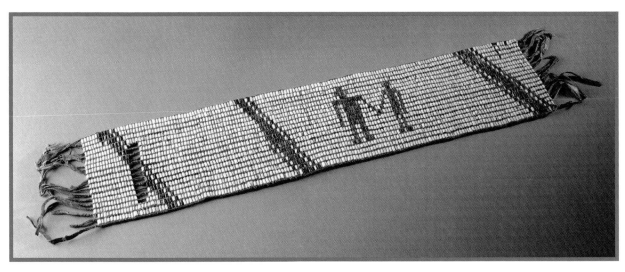

This wampum belt, made from strings of beads, is believed to have been given to William Penn by the Lenape as a gift in 1682. Penn, who settled the colony of Pennsylvania in Lenape territory, is often remembered for having treated the Lenape with respect.

# Appearance and Clothing

Like their diet, the clothing of the Lenape changed with the seasons. When it was warm, men and older boys wore breechcloths. Women and girls wore skirts that reached below the knee and were often decorated with porcupine quills or painted with pigments. It was common for both men and women to wear nothing above the waist in warm weather. Boys under the age of six often wore no clothes at all.

When the weather grew cold, both men and women wore leggings and layers of fur, sometimes in the form of cloaks or capes.

17

18    The Lenape painted different patterns of shapes and lines on their faces with clay, berries, and other materials.

Skins from bears, beavers, wolves, and many other animals were used for warmth. While going barefoot was common in the warmer seasons, during the winter the Lenape wore moccasins made of animal hide to protect their feet.

The Lenape painted their bodies and faces with clay, berries, ground rock, and other materials. Tattooing was also a common practice. By pricking the skin with a needle and rubbing in charcoal, the Lenape created patterns of dots, circles, lines, and other geometric designs on their faces, arms, chests, and legs.

Women often wore their hair long and loose or simply tied back. Men had more varied hairstyles. Some men plucked their hair from the forehead to the crown, leaving the remaining strands long. Others removed all hair except for a patch on the top of the head. Other men wore one side long and braided with feathers and kept the other side bare.

# Family Structure and Government

In the Lenape social system, family ties were determined through the mother and her female ancestors. When a man and a woman married, the man sometimes went to live in the lodge of his wife's mother. If people divorced, which was permitted in Lenape society, the children would remain with their mother in the mother's lodge.

Lenape children were born into one of three clans: wolf, turtle, or turkey. A Lenape child belonged to the clan of his or her mother.

The clan system helped to bring order to Lenape society in many ways. Clans provided an important sense of connection between different groups of Lenape. For example, when the Lenape traveled for trade, hunting, or visiting, the visitor could find members of his or her own clan in each village. Children would be cared for within their clan if they lost their parents. Two members of a certain clan were not allowed to marry since they were considered relatives. This system created a wide network of support and shared responsibility for all Lenape.

A Lenape chief, or *sakima*, was appointed from a selection of men. These men were usually the brothers of respected elder women. Generally, the Lenape worked together to make decisions through group discussions. Advice of the *sakima*, elder tribe members, medicine people, warriors, or skilled toolmakers, was appropriate for each situation discussed at a meeting. In times of war, the *sakima* was sometimes replaced by a war leader. However, this was only a temporary position.

This 1735 portrait of Lappawinsoe, a Lenape chief, was commissioned by John Penn, one of William Penn's sons. Lappawinsoe is believed to have signed the Walking Purchase in 1737, a treaty in which the Lenape lost a large area of land to William Penn's sons.

# Three

## Lenape Spirits and Religion

## Spirits

The Lenape believed that nature was full of spirits. These spirits were called *manetuwak*. The Lenape talked to the spirits as if they were members of their families. They spoke to the moon, the stars, the trees, the rivers, the animals, and the plants around them. It was important for the Lenape to live in harmony with the *manetuwak*. They believed that if they did not make peace with the spirits, their hunts would go badly, crops would not grow, the rain would not fall, and people would become sick.

The Great Spirit of the Lenape is called He Who Created Us By His Thoughts. According to a Lenape creation myth, this spirit created the world and all things in it. The Lenape believe that the universe is divided into twelve levels of heaven. He Who Created Us By His Thoughts exists in the uppermost twelfth level of the universe, called the Land of Good Spirits. People live in the first level, or lowest level of the universe. When a Lenape person died, his or her spirit would join the creator's spirit in the beautiful Land of the Good Spirits. The Lenape believed that the stars of the Milky Way were the footprints of spirits on their way to heaven.

This mask represents Living Solid Face, one of the most important Lenape spirits. Living Solid Face was the protector of animals. During special ceremonies, a Lenape man danced while wearing a mask like this to call on the power of the spirit.

The Lenape also believed that each of the four directions on Earth had its own spirit. The North was called Grandfather Winter, the East was called Grandfather Dawn, and the West was known as Grandfather Sunset. The spirit of the South was called Grandmother Where It Is Warm. This spirit, along with a spirit called Mother Corn, was especially important to the Lenape because of their reliance on seasonal crops for survival. Mother Corn controlled the spirits of all plants and worked in harmony with a spirit called Mother Earth, who gave nourishment to all living creatures.

One of the most important Lenape spirits was a spirit called Living Solid Face. This spirit was the guardian of all animals. Lenape hunters were

Turtle-shell rattles were used in many Lenape ceremonies. In some cases, they were shaken to direct attention to a speaker. In other situations, they were used as musical instruments to keep time with a drumbeat. They were also sometimes shaken to help heal a sick person.

especially respectful of him. To keep a balance with nature, hunters only killed as many animals as they needed in order to survive. To respect Living Solid Face, the hunters were expected to release the spirits of the animals they killed, returning them to the spirit world so they could be reborn. If a hunter displeased Living Solid Face, he might face bad luck at his next hunt. In extreme cases, Living Solid Face might even scare the hunter to death. In special ceremonies, a Lenape man dressed in a wooden mask and a bearskin to portray this spirit. The man also carried a rattle made of a snapping turtle shell, an animal skin bag, and a long wooden staff. It was believed that when a man dressed as Living Solid Face during this ceremony, he acquired the spirit's power and could cure diseases. The Lenape believed that as a man acquired this power, the spirit could be seen behind him.

The Lenape also believed in spirits known as Thunder Beings who were responsible for rain and lightning. Some Lenape say the Thunder Beings were giant eagle-like creatures with human heads. They always carried bows and arrows and would shoot them down from the sky in the form of lightning, which could shatter trees and cause fires. Thunder Beings watered the earth and protected the Lenape from an evil spirit called Great Horned Serpent, who lived in rivers and lakes.

MANETTO INDIANORUM,

This image is believed to represent the Great Horned Serpent, an evil Lenape spirit who lived in the water. Experts have estimated that it was carved over the doorway of a Lenape house before 1831.

# Dreams

The Lenape paid special attention to dreams. They believed that the spirits around them would often speak to them through their dreams. A Lenape person visited by powerful animal spirits in their dreams and visions could become an important leader of their people. Some even became medicine people. Parents sometimes had their sons stay out in the woods overnight, hoping that the spirits would visit them in powerful dreams.

26

# Ceremonies

Ceremonies and rituals were a way for the Lenape to maintain proper harmony with the spirits around them. The most important ceremony of the year was The Big House Ceremony, which lasted for 12 days. The purpose of the ceremony was to unite Lenape people, prevent sickness and disaster, thank the Creator for the crops raised that year, and to defend the tribe against harmful forces.

The Lenape held other ceremonies to satisfy spirits that watched over animals and to ensure or celebrate the harvest. These ceremonies included ritual dances, singing, and music played with animal hide drums and turtle-shell rattles. They often included the reciting of different dreams or visions. The Lenape also offered the spirits burnt meat, cedar leaves, and tobacco.

# Myths

The Lenape had a rich oral tradition in which myths, legends, folktales, and history were handed down from generation to generation. Storytelling was an important part of daily life. It was used to pass on knowledge about proper behavior, spiritual beliefs, practical matters, and many other aspects of Lenape culture.

Some Lenape myths involved explanations for how the Lenape people were created. The following creation myth, probably collected between 1641 and 1655, explains the origin of the world and human nature. Since the Lenape clan system was linked to animals, explaining the close ties between animals and humans was of great importance. This tale also shows how women were often powerful figures in Lenape myths.

*At first, the whole world was entirely covered by water. Then a beautiful woman with a very large belly came down from heaven and settled onto the water. Land began to appear beneath her, where she sat, and more and more land emerged until it reached as far as the eye could see. Plants began to grow on the land. More plants grew until the once dry land was full of trees and vegetation as it is now.*

*Then the beautiful woman gave birth to three creatures: a deer, a bear, and a wolf. She nursed the three animals until they were grown and she stayed on Earth, living with them. It is from these animals and their beautiful mother that all other animals and human beings came.*

*When all the creatures we know today were finally made perfect, and when they could live by themselves, the great mother rejoiced and ascended back up to heaven, where she now stays in goodness and in love with the Great Spirit. It is because we are all born of the three original animals that all people have the nature of one of them. We are like the deer: timid and innocent. We are like the bear: brave, vengeful, and just. Or we are like the wolf: cunning and bloodthirsty.*

# Another Creation Myth

Another Lenape creation story, from 1679, was told by an 80-year-old man named Tantaque. It offers a different explanation for the creation of Earth and the origin of the first people. Tantaque illustrated the story by drawing on the floor with a piece of coal he had taken out of a fire.

He first drew a circle, a little oval, to which he made four paws, or feet, a head and a tail. "This," said he, "is a tortoise, lying in the water around it ... this ... is all water, and so at first was the world... when the tortoise gradually raised its back up high, and the water ran off it, and thus the earth became dry ... and there grew a tree in the middle of the earth, and the root of this tree sent forth a sprout beside it and there grew upon it a man, who was the first male. This man was then alone ... but the tree bent over until its top touched the earth, and there shot therein another root, from which came forth another sprout, and there grew upon it the woman, and from these two are all men produced."

This Lenape story contains the image of a flooded world—an image which is also found in many other creation myths from different cultures around the world.

# Four

## Encounters with Europeans

## First Contacts

In 1524, the French government asked Giovanni da Verrazano, a respected Italian seaman, to find a shorter route from Europe to Asia to make trading easier. Many scholars believe he was the first European explorer to have contact with the Lenape. Verrazano sailed to the New World and entered New York Bay. He claimed the surrounding land for the king of France, calling it New France.

In 1609, English explorer Henry Hudson also sailed to North America, looking for a shorter passage from Europe to Asia. He claimed lands in New York for the Dutch. The Dutch called the Lenape homeland New Netherland and gave a group of Dutch merchants the right to set up forts and control trade there.

No one knows for sure how the Lenape and other native people felt about their first encounters with Europeans. All of the written accounts of these encounters come from Europeans and only offer one side of the story. However, it is clear that from the time the Europeans came in contact with the Lenape, there were conflicts between the two groups.

In September 1609, Henry Hudson explored the Hudson River, which was later named for him. He claimed the surrounding land for the Dutch. In the following years, many Dutch settlers came to live in Lenape territory.

# Conflicts Over Property

In 1624, a large number of Dutch colonists came into Lenape territory. Many families established homes and communities in different parts of New Netherland. One of these communities was a trading post at the southern tip of Manhattan Island called New Amsterdam. This area would later become known as New York City. As more and more settlers came to live in the Lenape homeland, conflicts quickly grew.

European colonists wanted to own land and refused to recognize any rights the Lenape had to it. Some of them tried to buy this land from the Lenape legally, while others simply seized it without paying for it. Some settlers even cheated the Lenape, tricking them out of their land. Very few Lenape spoke European languages and few Europeans spoke the language of the Lenape. This created a problem in discussions about land deals and ownership rights.

The European settlers were familiar with the idea of land ownership. It was a central part of their lives, developed over hundreds of years and built into their laws and customs. For the Lenape, however, these European rules made little sense. The Lenape did not understand the concept of one person owning vast amounts of land, outlawing hunting, and requiring rent from those farming on the property. To the Europeans, the sale of land often meant the seller was giving up hunting, farming, and grazing rights for all time.

From the records of the time, it is not clear what selling land meant to the Lenape. The Lenape often expected to continue hunting, gathering, and living on land the Europeans claimed had been sold to them.

In 1624, Dutch colonist Peter Minuit purchased New York for only $24 from the Native Americans living there. It is believed that the Native Americans mistakenly thought they were selling the colonists their permission to use the land. This letter from colonist Peter Schagen to the Dutch government, dated November 5, 1626, is the only known written record of the sale.

33

# Conflicts Over Resources

The Europeans placed a high value on furs. By the 1600s, there were few animals left to hunt in Europe. After Henry Hudson reported large numbers of beaver, otter, fox, and deer available in the New World, Dutch ships and fur traders came to live in Lenape territory in increasing numbers.

The fur trade forever changed life as the Lenape knew it. The traders brought terrible diseases with them that the Lenape had never known, such as tuberculosis, influenza, and smallpox. The Lenape and other Native Americans had little resistance to these new diseases. Many Native Americans died from them.

Before the Europeans came, the Lenape had lived in harmony with nature for hundreds of years. The Lenape respected the spirits and forces of nature, taking only the natural resources they needed to survive. They chose to live in harmony with their environment because their lives depended on the yearly renewal of plants and animals around them.

The European settlers had a very different view of their relationship to nature. They saw themselves as the most important creatures on Earth. They considered the native people to be lesser beings. The Europeans wanted to take as much as they could from resources within the Lenape and other native homelands as quickly as possible. The Europeans saw the animals and forests as resources they could exploit to create wealth. This view of nature was very different from the Lenape's. The Europeans disrupted the balance with nature that the Lenape maintained in order to survive.

The fur trade introduced many new goods to the Lenape, such as iron axes, needles, knives, pots, guns, and woven cloth. The Lenape came to prefer these tools over their own. The Europeans' metal knives and axes remained sharp and did not break as easily as the Lenape's stone tools had. Woven cloth was more comfortable than the Lenape furs were when wet and metal pots lasted far longer than the Lenape pots made from clay. As the Lenape's desire for these European items grew, they hunted more and more. They traded animal pelts for the European's metal goods and cloth, as well as for alcohol, glass beads, and other prized items that the Europeans had introduced to them.

European settlers introduced the Lenape to beads, which eventually replaced porcupine quills in Lenape crafts. The Lenape used the beads to make jewelry and to decorate bags and clothing. They also traded the beads for other goods.

Huge numbers of animals were hunted and killed in the early decades of the fur trade. Great numbers of beaver, deer, elk, and otter were hunted for their hides. As the Lenape spent more time hunting, trapping, and preparing furs for trade, they became more dependent on European goods. In just a few decades, the fur trade had upset the traditional balance the Lenape had held with nature for so long.

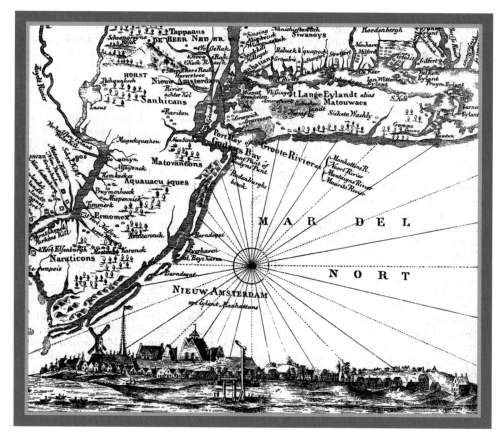

This 1656 map shows the Dutch colony of New Netherland. Established in 1624, the colony began with 30 families and grew into a large, successful settlement. Pictured at the bottom of the map is a view of New Amsterdam, an important settlement in what is now called New York City.

The fur trade also caused many conflicts among neighboring native tribes. The tribes competed for European goods, hunting farther and farther from their lodges. During this period, the Lenape's relationship with the Susquehannock and the Haudenosaunee grew difficult. The introduction of new European weapons, especially rifles, led to the loss of many more lives in the fighting between tribes.

Overhunting eventually led to the collapse of the fur trade. This left the Lenape in a difficult position. They were now dependent on European goods, but were left without the animals they needed to trade for them.

Alcohol, introduced by explorers and traders, became the cause of many conflicts during this period. When rum and beer were introduced, the Lenape and other native peoples had no understanding of their possible negative effects. Violence and addiction were two ongoing problems that alcohol brought to many Native American communities.

# Conflicts Over Land Use

Swedish explorers had established the New Sweden colony along the southern portion of the Delaware River and Bay in 1638. However, they were at constant battle with the Dutch over that land. The Lenape's relations with the Dutch and the Swedes grew worse as each group competed for resources. The Europeans' animals often fed on Lenape crops. Sometimes, the Lenape killed these animals for food, as their supply had grown scarce from overhunting.

The Europeans saw the Lenape presence as an obstacle in the way of settling the new land. The governor of New Sweden, John Printz, said of the Lenape, "Nothing would be better than a couple of hundred soldiers should be sent here and kept here until we broke the necks of all of them . . . and also we could take possession of the places . . . that the savages possess."

By the 1640s, a Dutchman named William Kieft had control of New Netherland. His actions began a difficult period for the Lenape. For several years, he had demanded that the Lenape pay taxes for using the land now inhabited by colonists. He tried to punish the Lenape who did not pay. Kieft also allowed the colonists to permit their animals to ruin Lenape crops. In 1643, he ordered the massacre of more than a hundred Lenape while they were sleeping. One Dutch eyewitness, David Pieterz de Vries, described the murder of parents, children, and infants. Some were drowned while others were hacked to death and tossed in a fire.

This massacre forced the Lenape to band together to fight the Dutch. The Lenape killed men, burned the colonists' houses, and killed or captured women, children, and farm animals. The colonists responded with more violence against the Lenape. Thousands of Europeans and Native Americans died during this period.

The Dutch colony was weakened by these conflicts. The English took over New Netherland in 1664. It then became known as New York. The English were even more determined to acquire land than the Dutch and Swedes had been. By the time the Dutch had given up their claim to New Netherland, English colonies stretched from north of Florida to south of Canada. British settlers had overrun the Lenape homeland.

# English Settlement

In 1681, English settler William Penn was granted a large area of land by King Charles II. Penn called this territory Pennsylvania. The king gave this land to Penn to settle a debt owed to Penn's father. This land was part of Lenapehoking.

Penn was a Quaker, a member of a religious group that did not believe in traditional Christianity. Penn wanted his territory to be a place where people of different religious beliefs could live peacefully. Unlike many other colonists, Penn intended to pay the Lenape for their territory. Some historians believe he was acting out of respect for the Native Americans. Others think he wanted to make

William Penn named his colony Pennsylvania, which means "Penn's woods." This 1832 portrait of Penn was done by artist Henry Inman after Penn's death.

sure they could not later claim they owned the land the king had granted him.

While Penn was kind to the Lenape and truly interested in their customs, language, and history, he was more interested in setting up his colony. His desires for the land eventually created conflict with the Lenape. Penn needed to sell the land to colonists to establish his new territory. The Lenape needed the undeveloped land to hunt, gather, and farm in order to survive.

This 1771 painting, called *Penn's Treaty with the Indians*, shows William Penn and other settlers meeting with a group of Native Americans. Thomas Penn, William Penn's son, had artist Benajmin West create this painting to show the friendship between the cultures at the time the Walking Purchase was signed.

# The Walking Purchase

William Penn died in 1718. Almost two decades later, his sons John and Thomas cheated the Lenape out of 1,200 square miles (3,108 square km) of their territory in what is known as the Walking Purchase. Penn's sons found a copy of a document signed by both William Penn and three Lenape chiefs about 50 years earlier. The document claimed that the Lenape had given Penn and his heirs all of the land west of a specific point in Delaware to as far as a man could walk in a day and a half. At the time the document was signed, the Lenape believed that this would cover about 30 square miles (77.7 square km).

In the summer of 1737, the Penn brothers and other Pennsylvanians decided to see how far this land actually extended. After clearing a trail and training walkers and a runner to travel the distance, the English claimed more than twice the distance the Lenape had expected. However, the brothers could not produce the original deed to support their claim. The Haudenosaunee, or the powerful Six Nations Iroquois Confederacy, forced the Lenape to give up the land. The Iroquois wanted to protect their own alliance with the English government.

# Loss of the Homeland

Many scholars believe that there could have been 23,000 or more Lenape living in Lenapehoking before the coming of the Europeans. Within one hundred years, the Lenape may have lost as many as 90 percent of their people. This loss of life was caused by disease, war, forced removal from their homeland, and the disruption of their traditional way of life. Much of the Lenape cultural history was lost as beloved family members, skilled toolmakers, warriors, medicine people, storytellers, chiefs, elders, and many others died.

The ancestral homeland had been lost to all but a small number of surviving Lenape. Some remained in remote areas and some intermarried and settled with Europeans. For most Lenape, however, a long westward exodus had begun. The Lenape divided into different groups as they moved to different areas of North America. Those from the central and southern portion of the ancestral lands were now mostly called Delaware. Those from the north were mostly called Munsee.

Some Munsee traveled northwest along what is now the New York-Pennsylvania border. Many surviving Delaware went to the Susquehanna and Ohio River Valleys, where the abundant natural resources allowed them to hunt, gather, farm, and raise livestock. Another group settled near Wyoming, Pennsylvania.

In 1740, missionaries from Germany bought some of the land the Lenape had lost in the Walking Purchase. A number of Lenape converted to Christianity and settled with or near the missionaries. The missionaries taught them reading, writing, European farming methods, and other skills.

From 1756 through 1764, the Delaware were forced farther west as their homeland was taken over by European settlers. The Delaware fought against the British in the French and Indian War (1754), the struggle between the British and French for control of North America. When the British defeated the French in 1758, the

During the 1740s, a group of missionaries known as the Moravians worked to convert the Lenape to Christianity. Pictured above are missionaries preaching to a group of Native Americans, believed to be Lenape, in Pennsylvania around 1740.

Delaware lost even more land. The British had promised many Native Americans that they would keep white settlers out of Native American territory west of the Appalachian Mountains, but they broke their promise.

Pontiac, a war chief from the Ottawa tribe, brought together warriors from many tribes to try to drive the English back from Detroit and the Great Lakes region. The native warriors killed settlers and burned their farms. In response, the British destroyed Delaware settlements in Pennsylvania and Ohio. In 1764, the Delaware surrendered and white settlers flooded into the area west of the Appalachian and Allegheny Mountains.

# The American Revolutionary War

In 1775, the 13 American colonies united and revolted against their British rulers. This was a time of great uncertainty for the Native Americans. Many tribes, including some Delaware and some Munsee, sided with the British, who offered them a wealth of supplies. Other Delaware sided with the American colonists. Tired of the death and forced relocations caused by the war, some of the Delaware tried to avoid fighting altogether.

In 1778, the Continental Congress of the newly formed United States asked the Delaware for help. They wanted to be able to march through Delaware territory to attack the British. In return, the Congress offered to recognize the Delaware as the principal Indian nation in the Ohio Territory, making that territory the fourteenth state in the Union. As a part of the Union, the Delaware would be able to send representatives to the Congress to vote on important issues. A treaty was signed by Chief White Eyes and several American officials. This was known as the Treaty of Friendship, and was the first formal treaty ever signed between the United States and Native Americans.

Shortly after signing this treaty, Chief White Eyes died. Some people believe the Americans killed him. The Americans told the Delaware that Chief White Eyes had died from smallpox. The Americans never made the Treaty of Friendship a law, and the promise of the fourteenth state was never fulfilled.

In 1776, the Continental Congress of the United States of America signed the Declaration of Independence, separating the 13 American colonies from England. In the following years, some Delaware and Munsee found themselves fighting against each other in the American Revolutionary War.

The war dragged on. The Delaware who had sided with the Americans were starving and shortchanged of the basic supplies that the Americans had promised. Some of these Delaware joined the British. As groups of Delaware ended up on opposite sides in this war, they found themselves fighting against each other.

# The Gnadenhütten Massacre

In 1782, a group of colonists massacred more than 90 Delaware, Mahican, and possibly Wampanoag, who had converted to Christianity. Decades earlier, these people had settled with missionaries, and by this time, were living in Gnadenhütten, Ohio. These natives had refused to take sides in the revolution because of their Christian beliefs of pacifism, a commitment to living in peace. They were singing hymns and praying for mercy as the colonists attacked and killed them. As the news of this massacre spread among the Delaware and Munsee, many fled north in fear. Some eventually settled in Wisconsin. Others established homes in Ontario, Canada, where many of their descendants remain today.

# Final Removals

The Delaware and Munsee faced betrayal, starvation, exodus, war, and massacre. While some had escaped north, others continued to face suffering and death as they were pushed farther and farther west.

One group, sometimes known as the Absentee Delaware, were invited to what would later become Texas by the Mexican government. They linked themselves with other tribes, such as the Cherokee, the Creeks, and the Choctaw. Unfortunately for the Absentee Delaware, in 1845 Mexico lost control of Texas to the United States. The Absentee Delaware were forced out of the area. Many of them settled among other tribes, such as the Wichita, the Caddo, the Kiowa, and the Comanche.

Other Delaware had been pushed through Indiana and Missouri into Kansas. Some of the Delaware from Ontario and Wisconsin joined them and they created a community there. They built schools, houses, farms, and raised livestock. The U.S. government promised the Kansas Delaware "the undisturbed enjoyments" of the Kansas territory "against the claims and assaults of all and every other people." This promise was not kept. Railroad companies wanted their land and timber. American buffalo hunters slaughtered bison that the Delaware needed to survive. Other white settlers simply took their land with little regard for the Delaware. The U.S. government chose to ignore the white invasion and acts of violence. Native Americans were left to retreat, in fear for their lives. By 1867, after this final series of forced removals, and more deaths during the long journey, the Kansas Delaware arrived in the area now known as Oklahoma.

# Five

# The Lenape Today

## Continuing Struggles

Over about four centuries, the Lenape lost most of their people, land, family structure, and traditions. As Delaware and Munsee, many Lenape survivors struggled in poverty for generations. Some accepted the Christian religion and other practices of the white settlers. Others maintained traditional Lenape beliefs. Whatever choices they made, many of the surviving Lenape still remembered their old ways of working together for the good of their people.

During the late 1800s and early 1900s, Richard Adams was one of these people. Adams' father was a Delaware minister who had endured the tribe's removal from Kansas. Adams wrote several books about traditional Lenape folktales, history, and religious beliefs. He also fought for Delaware land rights and tribal recognition.

The work of Adams and others like him was very important in keeping Lenape traditions alive. In 1901, the U.S. government nullified all tribal governments of the Native Americans and forced them to accept allotted pieces of land. This meant that reservation lands were distributed to Native Americans at a set number of acres for each head of household. The remaining lands were sold

This is John Anderson, a Delaware from Dewey, Oklahoma, wearing traditional Lenape clothing. The photograph was taken in Bartlesville, Oklahoma, around 1910.

off to non-natives. According to some estimates, 82,000,000 acres (33,184,222 ha) of reservation land were lost in this way.

In the nineteenth and twentieth centuries, both Canadian and United States government policies forced Native American children to receive their education in boarding schools, sometimes hundreds of miles away from their homes. This helped put an end to many Lenape traditions. Children were forced to speak English and learn the Christian religion. They were often punished for speaking their native language or for practicing their own religious beliefs.

Some Delaware fought to be recognized by the U.S. government. The Delaware in eastern Oklahoma avoided allotment at first because they had bought their land from the Cherokee Nation 40 years earlier. They were living among the Cherokee, but as a separate tribe. The U.S. courts ruled against them, however, and they were forced into allotment. The U.S. government no longer recognized the Delaware who lived among the Cherokee in eastern Oklahoma as a separate tribe. This group, like many others, continued to fight for their tribal identity and legal rights.

## The Lenape Now

Today, the Delaware and Munsee live in many places in the United States and Canada. Small numbers survived in New Jersey, New York, Pennsylvania, and Kansas. Some married members of white communities. Some Lenape descendants are in Canada, at reserves in Moraviantown and Muncey, Ontario. Others, many of whom have married members of other tribes, live with the Iroquois on the Six Nations Reserve, which is also in Ontario.

In the United States, there is a Munsee population at the Stockbridge-Munsee Reservation in Wisconsin. They were officially recognized as a tribe in 1938, and used funds they received from the government to purchase a 15,000-acre reservation in addition to property they owned individually. There are large groups of Delaware in the Anadarko and Bartlesville areas of Oklahoma. Many have taken on official names. The Delaware tribe of Western Oklahoma now calls itself the Delaware Nation. After various struggles, the Delaware tribe of Eastern Oklahoma regained federal recognition in 1996.

Many important Delaware leaders have worked hard to keep the traditions of their Lenape heritage alive. In 1930, a Delaware named Walks With Daylight worked with a woman named Gladys Tantaquidgeon to preserve information about Delaware spiritual and curing practices, especially about using plants and trees to create medicine. Tantaquidgeon was an anthropologist, a special kind of scientist who studies other cultures. Together, Walks With Daylight and Tantaquidgeon saved valuable information about Lenape traditions.

Nora Thompson Dean, another Lenape descendant, was one of the last speakers of the Lenape dialect known as Unami. Until her death in 1984, she worked tirelessly to teach people about Lenape language and traditions. A gifted storyteller, she helped keep many of the stories of her people alive for generations to come. Her cousin,

Lucy Parks Blalock, took over the mission until her own death in 2000. Dedicated scholars like James Rementer are now continuing the task of keeping Lenape traditions alive through the Lenape Language Project.

In 1979, Nora Thompson Dean wrote *Lenape Language Lessons*. She also recorded tapes of the proper translations of important Lenape words. Her efforts have helped keep the language of the Lenape from being forgotten.

During the 1980s and 1990s, speakers of other Lenape dialects worked to preserve their language for future generations. They helped John O'Meara, a scientist who studies languages, create a Delaware-English dictionary.

In 1992, the Stomp Dance, a group of traditional Lenape social dances, was revived among the Delaware of eastern Oklahoma. The dance inspired hope for the revival of other Lenape customs. A fall gathering was also held in 1992 in Moraviantown, Ontario. Since that year, this gathering has been held annually, bringing together Lenape from many places. Members of this dispersed group unite to honor their traditional ways through singing, dancing, drumming, offering prayers, and lighting fires.

In May of 2003, a group of Delaware tribal members gathered at Ellis Island in New York City. Several years earlier, construction workers had uncovered skeletal remains in the area.

This photograph of Lucy Parks Blalock was taken on October 20, 1977 at the State Museum of Pennsylvania. She holds a beaded belt that she made in 1929.

Scientists studied the bones and linked them to the Lenape. The Delaware tribal members reburied these bones in a special ceremony, returning their ancestors to Earth and to the spirit world.

The Lenape have survived countless efforts to end their traditions and their tribe. Even after being scattered for hundreds of

years on trails not of their own choosing, the Lenape celebrate their ancient heritage. Although separated from one another, the surviving Lenape work together to keep their culture alive.

Descendants of the Lenape work to maintain their tradition of living in harmony with nature.

# Timeline

| | |
|---|---|
| **13,000 to 40,000 years ago** | Ancient ancestors of the Native Americans travel from Asia to North America. |
| **1000 A.D.** | The Lenape farm, hunt, and gather in the area currently known as the Middle Atlantic region of the United States. |
| **1524** | Giovanni da Verrazano sails into what is now New York Harbor. This is the first recorded contact between the Lenape and Europeans. |
| **1609** | Henry Hudson sails up the river that was later named for him. Soon, Dutch fur traders arrive in Lenape territory in increasing numbers. Within the next several decades, settlers from many European countries arrive in the colonies. |
| **1710** | As many as 90 percent of the Lenape have died from illness, war, forced relocation, and disruption of their way of life. |

| | |
|---|---|
| **1737** | The Lenape lose most of their remaining land in eastern Pennsylvania in the Walking Purchase. |
| **1778** | Chief White Eyes signs the first written treaty between a Native American group and a U.S. government. |
| **1782** | Many Delaware and other Native Americans are murdered in Gnadenhütten, Ohio. |
| **1828–70** | Following forced removals from Kansas and Texas, two groups of Lenape settle in what is now Oklahoma. Others settle in Wisconsin. |
| **1887–1907** | The U.S. government sells off Indian territory and reservation lands through allotment. As a result, many Native Americans face homelessness and poverty. |
| **2003** | Delaware tribe members preside over the reburial of ancient Lenape remains discovered on Ellis Island at the end of the twentieth century. |

# Glossary

**alewives** (AYL-wivez) Small fish abundant along the Atlantic coast of North America.

**Algonquian** (al-GON-kee-an) A family of American Indian languages. Not all speakers of Algonquian languages could understand each other, although some of the languages had words in common.

**allotment** (uh-LOT-muhnt) The assignment of portions of land.

**ancestral** (an-SESS-trul) Members of a family who lived a long time ago.

**anthropologist** (an-thruh-POL-uh-jist) A scientist who studies human cultures of the past and present.

**breechcloths** (BREECH-clothz) Long, narrow pieces of animal skins pulled up between a man's legs and fastened with a narrow belt around the waist.

**clan** (KLAN) A subdivision of a tribal society made up of families. The members of a clan trace their descent from a common ancestor.

**crown** (KROUN) The top of a person's head.

**dialect** (DYE-uh-lekt) A form of a language shared by a group that is usually understandable by other speakers of that language. Pronunciation, grammar, and vocabulary may differ among dialects.

**exodus** (EK-suh-duhss) The departure of a large group from their place of residence. An exodus sometimes occurs after a disaster caused by human or natural forces.

**exploit** (ek-SPLOIT) To make use of unfairly for one's own advantage.

**Haudenosaunee** (ho-dee-noh-SHO-nee) The Native American word for the people of the Iroquois Confederacy. This group is often known by the French name, Iroquois.

**hearths** (HARTHS) Fireplaces.

**invasion** (in-VAY-shun) An act of disturbing or intruding upon.

**Lenapehoking** (luh-nah-pay-HAWK-king) Nora Thompson Dean, one of the last speakers of the Unami dialect, created this term in 1984 for the area where the Lenape lived prior to European contact. This term is used by scholars and Delawares today.

*manetuwak* (ma-ni-TOO-uk) The Lenape word for spirits.

**missionaries** (MI-shuh-ner-eez) People sent to spread a religious faith among others.

**mortar** (MOR-tur) A deep bowl used with a pestle for crushing things.

**nullified** (NUH-luh-fide) To make of no value or consequence.

**pelts** (PELTZ) Animal skins with the hair or fur still on them.

**pigments** (PIG-muhnts) Substances that give color to something.

**reservation** (reh-zuhr-VAY-shuhn) An area of land that the U.S. government allowed Native Americans to keep for their own use. Many Native Americans ended up on reservations far from their original homelands. In Canada, reservations are called "reserves."

*sakima* (sah-KEE-mah) A chief of a band of Lenape. The position traditionally passed along sister-brother ties through the mother's clan. A *sakima* was chosen because of leadership skills. War chiefs were appointed in times of conflict.

**shad** (SHAD) A small, herring-like fish found in the waters around North America and Europe.

**stripped** (STRIPPD) Having had outer layers pulled, torn, or taken off.

**timber** (TIM-bur) Cut wood used for building.

**tradition** (TRUH-di-shuhn) A belief or custom handed down from one generation to another.

*xwas-kweem* (XUS-kweem) The Lenape word for corn.

**wigwams** (WIG-wamz) Huts of some Native Americans, typically having an arched framework of poles overlaid with bark or hides.

# Resources

## BOOKS

Adams, Richard C. *Legends of the Delaware Indians and Picture Writing.* Syracuse, NY: Syracuse University Press, 1997.

Goddard, Ives. "Delaware." In *Handbook of North American Indians.* Vol. 15, edited by R. H. Ives Goddard III, pp. 213-39. Washington, D.C.: Smithsonian Institution Press, 1978.

Grumet, Robert S. *The Lenapes.* New York: Chelsea House Publishers, 1990.

Harrington, Mark Raymond. *Religion and Ceremonies of the Lenape.* New York: Museum of the American Indian, 1921.

Kraft, Herbert C. *The Lenape-Delaware Indian Heritage: 10,000 B.C. to A.D. 2000.* Lenape Books, 2001.

Myers, Albert Cook, Ed. *William Penn's Own Account of the Lenni Lenape or Delaware Indians* (Revised Edition). Somerset, NJ: The Middle Atlantic Press, 1970.

Tantaquidgeon, Gladys. *Folk Medicine of the Delaware and Related Algonkian Indians.* Harrisburg, PA: The Pennsylvania Historical and Museum Commission, 1972.

Weslager, C. A. *The Delaware Indians: A History.* New Brunswick, NJ: Rutgers University Press, 2000.

# WEB SITES

Due to the changing nature of Internet links, PowerKids Press has developed an online list of Web sites related to the subject of this book. This site is updated regularly. Please use this link to access the list:

http://www.powerkidslinks.com/lna/lenape

# Index